CHRISTIAN CONDUCT

OR, THE WAY TO HEAVEN

CHARLES E. ORR

ALICIA EDITIONS

CONTENTS

Preface — 1

PART I

Introduction — 5
1. Christian Experience — 11
2. Repentance — 13
3. Regeneration — 17
4. Sanctification — 19

PART II

1. Christian Conduct — 35
2. Christianity in Home Life — 44
3. Husband's Duty to His Wife — 46
4. Wife's Duty to Her Husband — 49
5. Parents' Duty to Their Children — 52
6. Children's Duty to Their Parents — 56
7. Servants' Duty to Their Masters — 58
8. Masters' Duty to Their Servants — 59
9. Christianity in Public Life — 62
10. The Effect of Christianity on Habit — 69
11. Christianity in Dress — 73

12. Christianity Separates from the World	79
13. What Christians Must Not Do	85
14. What Christians Must Do Christianity	87 89

PREFACE

"Only let your conduct be as it becometh the gospel of Christ."[1]

We kindly ask the reader to compare the words of this booklet with the Word of God. What I have written has not been with an unkind nor unfriendly spirit, and I hope no one will take offense. My object has been to exalt Christianity to her rightful throne and plainly mark out the Christian way, that we all may live to the glory of God and to gain a home in heaven.

Your in Christian hope and love,
Charles E. Orr

1. Philippians 1 (27) Only let your conversation be as it becometh the gospel of Christ: that whether I come and see you, or else be absent, I may hear of your affairs, that ye stand fast in one spirit, with one mind striving together for the faith of the gospel;

PART I

INTRODUCTION

My Dear Friend:

We have come to have a short, earnest talk with you about heaven and the way that leads to that better land. In all the realm of thought and conversation there is no sweeter theme than that of heaven. Oh, what pleasantness there is associated with the thoughts and hopes of spending an eternity in the blissful fields of that glory world. As we look upon the pale, lifeless form of some dear one whose spirit has flown away, what a comfort comes to our sorrowing breast when we have reason to hope they have gone to heaven.

There are frequent occurrences along the journey of life which remind us that we are only pilgrims, traveling to an eternal beyond, to which we may be called any day. It may be we have been in imminent danger and narrowly escaped the blow that severs the thread of life. It may be the sick chamber. It may be the news of someone who has departed this life, or the vacant seats around our own hearthstone. All these remind us that it is "appointed unto men once to die."[1] We cannot forbear remarking here, "Be ye also ready: for in such an hour as ye think not"[2] the call may come to you. Surely you can not fail to comprehend the necessity of living every hour in such a way that, should the summons come, you could

> *Go softly and peacefully to rest,*
> *Like slumb'ring childhood from*
>   *task set free,*
> *Or evening breeze 'mid orchard*
>   *branches*
> *Separating blossoms from the tree.*

There are no aching hearts in heaven; no troubled breasts nor careworn brows. There is no sorrow there; neither pain nor tears. With such a place of eternal blessedness set before us, is it not wisdom to "give diligence to make your calling and election sure"[3]?

The Savior said, "In my Father's house are many mansions.... I go to prepare a place for you."[4] In the trying hours of life, when all seems to have forsaken us and the world appears unfriendly; life's burdens seem to be heavy, and a despondent feeling steals over our spirit, what a comfort to our trusting soul is the remembrance that there is a home prepared for us, "There the wicked cease from troubling; and there the weary be at rest."[5] There is room enough in heaven for all who will walk in the way that leads to that desired destination.

One night, while beholding the stars and thinking of that future home with our Father, we were given these lines:

> *Little stars in vault of heaven,*
> *Windows you appear to be*
> *Of my home, my home in glory.*
> *Draw the curtain back for me,*
> *Let me see the happy angels*
> *As they flit before the throne:*
> *If there's room for me in heaven*
> *Let me see my golden crown.*

I can see my Savior smiling,
In His hand a crown I see:
You may low'r the curtain softly
Since I know there's room for me.
All my soul is filled with glory,
Waves of peace sweep o'er my breast
When I think of going to heaven,
Where the weary are at rest.

While the thoughts of heaven are beautiful, there may be other thoughts that come like a blight over the spirit of many. Man is prone to draw a veil over the scenes that awaken thoughts of torment and woe; he invites thoughts of heaven, but banishes thoughts of hell. There is no pleasantness in the thoughts of eternal punishment. To think of spending an eternity in hell brings a terror to the soul. Whatever may be our feelings or thoughts, either heaven or hell shall be the eternal destination of all mankind. These two places are set before all who inhabit the earth. There is a way that leads from earth to heaven, and there is a way that leads from earth to hell. The way to heaven is called the way of life; the way to hell is called the way of death. These ways are set before every man, subject to his choice. He can take the way of life and gain heaven, or, he can take the way of death and make his bed in hell: "See, I have set before thee this day life and good, and death and evil.... I call heaven and earth to record this day against you, that I have set before you life and death, blessing and cursing: therefore choose life, that both thou and thy seed may live."[6]

It is not enough to say and to hope we are going to heaven; we must walk in the way that leads there, else our sayings and hopes will be in vain. Should you desire to go to a city, you must take the way that leads there. The way that leads to heaven is by the commandments of God. The Scriptures say: "Blessed are they that do his commandments, that they may have right to the tree of life, and may enter in through the gates into the city."[7] The Lord said: "Not every one that saith unto me, Lord, Lord, shall enter into the kingdom of heaven; but he that doeth the will of my Father which is in heaven."[8] The Bible is the book God has given to teach us the way to that goal of eternal peace and rest. There is no promise for us in that blessed volume, nor an intimation from which we can glean a ray of hope of gaining heaven, if we are knowingly violating any of its commandments (James 2:10). Only those who do

His commandments will enter through the gate into the city.

---

1. Hebrews 9 (27) And as it is appointed unto men once to die, but after this the judgment:
2. Matthew 24 (44) Therefore be ye also ready: for in such an hour as ye think not the Son of man cometh.
3. 2 Peter 1 (10) Wherefore the rather, brethren, give diligence to make your calling and election sure: for if ye do these things, ye shall never fall:
4. John 14 (2) In my Father's house are many mansions: if *it were* not *so*, I would have told you. I go to prepare a place for you.
5. Job 3 (17) There the wicked cease *from* troubling; and there the weary be at rest.
6. Deuteronomy 30 (15) See, I have set before thee this day life and good, and death and evil;

   ...

   (19) I call heaven and earth to record this day against you, *that* I have set before you life and death, blessing and cursing: therefore choose life, that both thou and thy seed may live:
7. Revelation 22 (14) Blessed *are* they that do his commandments, that they may have right to the tree of life, and may enter in through the gates into the city.
8. Matthew 7 (21) Not every one that saith unto me, Lord, Lord, shall enter into the kingdom of heaven; but he that doeth the will of my Father which is in heaven.

1

CHRISTIAN EXPERIENCE

An impure fountain does not send forth a pure stream; if we desire the stream to be pure, we must make the fountain pure. A holy and pure life naturally flows from a holy and pure heart. The wisdom of Solomon declares that "out of [the heart] are the issues of life."[1] The state or condition of the heart determines the manner of the life. One wiser than Solomon said: "For from within, out of the heart of men, proceed evil thoughts, adulteries, fornications, murders, thefts,"[2] etc. This saying illustrates the fact that the interior of man, or the heart, controls the exterior life. He further illustrates this by a cup and platter, which, he says, make clean on the inside, and the outside will be clean also

(Matthew 23:26). We shall take it for granted that every reader will agree with us when we say that Christian conduct necessitates Christian experience, and that where the former is wanting the latter is also wanting.

All men naturally are in sin, and consequently without Christian experience. Christianity is not a mere profession; it is a real inward, or heart, experience. In the plan of redemption we find certain things required of man in order that he may obtain this change in his moral condition. The principal thing required, and one which covers almost the whole, is—

---

1. Proverbs 4 (23) Keep thy heart with all diligence; for out of it *are* the issues of life.
2. Mark 7 (21) For from within, out of the heart of men, proceed evil thoughts, adulteries, fornications, murders, (22) Thefts, covetousness, wickedness, deceit, lasciviousness, an evil eye, blasphemy, pride, foolishness:

2

REPENTANCE

The Scripture tells us that repentance is a godly sorrow for sin, or, that "godly sorrow worketh repentance."[1] This is unlike the sorrow of the world. When a man has committed a wrong, and because this wrong is made public and he stands in danger of punishment by the law, he experiences a sorrow, his sorrow is only of the world. A child who, having disobeyed its parents, grieves through fear of punishment does not sorrow in a godly sense, and such sorrow contains but little or no merit. But when through force of temptation he disobeys his parents and sorrows because he has wronged a parent who loves him, he may be said to sorrow in a godly sense. When man wails and laments and seeks a Christian life merely to escape the torments of hell and to gain heaven, he is not truly penitent; but when in his very soul he grieves and sorrows because he has sinned against a God of love, having no thought of reward or punishment, but only sorrows because he has wronged a being who loves him—then he experiences a godly sorrow.

When a man sorrows in this manner he will turn away from his sins and forsake them. It must be obvious to the reader that man cannot be said to be truly sorry for his sins when he continues in them. But when in true penitence he turns away from his sinful life, God will pardon him. "Wash you, make you clean; put away the evil of your doings from before mine eyes; cease to do evil."[2] "Let the wicked forsake his way, and the unrighteous man his thoughts: and let him return unto the Lord, and he will have mercy upon him: and to our God, for he will abundantly pardon."[3]

When a man is truly sorrowful because he has sinned against God, he not only ceases to walk in the ways of sin, but he gladly makes right, as far as he can, all the wrongs he has done. We do a kind act toward God by doing it toward man, as Jesus says: "Inasmuch as ye have done it unto one of the least of these my brethren, ye have done it unto me"[4]; and we wrong God when we wrong our fellow man. Consequently, when a man truly repents, he will make right, as far as he can, all the wrongs he has done to his fellow man. We have this exemplified in the repentance of Zacchaeus when he said: "Behold, Lord, the half of my goods I give to the poor; and if I have taken any thing from any man by false accusation, I restore him four fold."[5] Jesus, upon seeing such penitence, said, "This day is salvation come to this house."[6] The law governing the restitutions of wrong in true repentance is recorded in Ezekiel 33:15: "If the wicked restore the pledge, give again that he had robbed, walk in the statutes of life, without committing iniquity; he shall surely live, he shall not die." The fruit of repentance is the forsaking of sin, of making right the wrongs we have done, of forgiving those who have wronged us, and of confessing our sinfulness to Him who sees and knows the heart; and, "If we confess our sins, he is faithful and just to forgive us our sins."[7] When pardoned, man experiences a change of affections; he experiences a change in his feelings and exterior life; he is no longer a sinner but a Christian. This experience is termed—

1. 2 Corinthians 7 (10) For godly sorrow worketh repentance to salvation not to be repented of: but the sorrow of the world worketh death.
2. Isaiah 1 (16) Wash you, make you clean; put away the evil of your doings from before mine eyes; cease to do evil;
3. Isaiah 55 (7) Let the wicked forsake his way, and the unrighteous man his thoughts: and let him return unto the Lord, and he will have mercy upon him; and to our God, for he will abundantly pardon.
4. Matthew 25 (40) And the King shall answer and say unto them, Verily I say unto you, Inasmuch as ye have done *it* unto one of the least of these my brethren, ye have done *it* unto me.
5. Luke 19 (8) And Zacchæus stood, and said unto the Lord; Behold, Lord, the half of my goods I give to the poor; and if I have taken any thing from any man by false accusation, I restore *him* fourfold.
6. Luke 19 (9) And Jesus said unto him, This day is salvation come to this house, forsomuch as he also is a son of Abraham.
7. 1 John 1 (9) If we confess our sins, he is faithful and just to forgive us *our* sins, and to cleanse us from all unrighteousness.

3

REGENERATION

The work of regeneration is effected by the grace of God: "By grace ye are saved."[1] When man complies with the requirements made of him by the Word of God, he will then through the act of faith, by the power and grace of God be born again or brought into spiritual life. He is a new creation. The guilt and condemnation of transgression is gone and he has peace with God. He is translated from the kingdom of darkness into that of God's dear Son. He has passed from death unto life. He is a branch of the vine, and now lives a sinless life. Although he enjoys much and experiences such peace and glory he learns there is an especial promise of the Father yet in store for him (Luke 24:49). He comes as an obedient child and pleads with the Father for the promise, and God, being more willing to give His children the Holy Spirit than parents are to give good gifts unto their children, sends the Holy Spirit in His cleansing power into his soul and he receives the glorious experience of—

---

1. Ephesians 2 (8) For by grace are ye saved through faith; and that not of yourselves: *it is* the gift of God:

4

SANCTIFICATION

It is our purpose in this booklet to write mainly upon the manner of a Christian's life, but we thought it well to set before the reader as briefly as possible the plan of redemption, or how we came into possession of the perfect fullness of the Christian experience.

Now it is sure we must be born again (John 3:1-7). But we do unmistakably find by searching the Scriptures that this is not all. The disciples as they journeyed with the Savior before his death enjoyed the experience of the new birth. We shall prove this by a few texts. In Matthew 16:15-16 Jesus is asking the disciples whom they believed him to be, and Peter making reply said, "Thou art the Christ, the Son of the living God." Again in John 6:69, Peter speaking to the Savior said, "We *believe and are sure* that thou art that Christ, the Son of the living God." Now by reading 1 John 5:1 we find what such believing effects: "Whosoever believeth that Jesus is the Christ is born of God."

From this we can safely conclude that the disciples were regenerated at the time they thus confessed their faith in Christ. Now I know we are in awful times of peril and deception, but it is perfectly safe to take the plain statements of God's Word. It is thought by some that none enjoyed the power of regeneration until after the resurrection, but we learn that He gave those who believed on Him power to become the sons of God before His crucifixion: "He came unto his own, and his own received him not. But as many as received him, to them gave he power to become the sons of God, even to them that believe on his name. Which were born, not of blood, nor of the will of the flesh, nor of the will of man, but of God."[1] The disciples believed on Him: they received Him and consequently were born of God. Jesus speaks to the seventy of their names being written in heaven (Luke 10:20). They were preaching the gospel, healing the sick, casting out devils, etc., and surely they were sons of God by the new birth.

But we obviously find yet an element in their nature discordant with the nature of their Savior. It is in the plan of redemption that we be restored to the image or nature of God. Christ came in the nature of God, and we in the fullness of His salvation are partakers of His nature; i.e., we are of a like nature with Him: "The disciple is not above his master: but every one that is perfect shall be as his master."[2] Not in outward life only shall we be like Jesus, but in our very nature: "Herein is our love made perfect, that we may have boldness in the day of judgment: because as he is, so are we in this world."[3] From this text we learn that it is not only in heaven that we shall in our nature be like Jesus, but like Him in this world as well. We are to be perfect in love as He is. For proof of this we shall quote Matthew 5:48: "Be ye therefore perfect, even as your Father which is in heaven is perfect." By reading a few above verses we find there is a perfection of love, and such a perfection can only result from a Christlike nature. In the fullness of salvation we are as merciful in our nature as God is merciful: "Be ye therefore merciful, as your Father also is merciful."[4] We are holy like

Him: "Be ye holy; for I am holy." We are to be righteous as He: "Little children, let no man deceive you: he that doeth righteousness is righteous, even as he [God] is righteous."[5] We are to be pure as our Savior: "And every man that hath this hope in him purifieth himself, even as he is pure."[6] We as Christians are to be one, as Christ and God are one: "And the glory which thou gavest me I have given them; that they may be one, even as we are one."[7] From the above texts we unmistakably learn that Christians in the "uttermost salvation" are holy, righteous, and pure in their nature as God is. They are as perfect in love and merciful in their nature as He is. They are naturally one even as the Father and the Son are one.

We have heretofore by a few texts positively proved that the disciples during the ministry of Christ were converted, regenerated, or born again. Now we will as positively prove by their actions or manner of life that there was an element in their nature unlike their Master. In reading Mark 9:33-34, we find the Savior rebuking the disciples because they had disputed among themselves, who should be greatest. Here we discover an element of pride or love of preeminence in the nature of the disciples, which is not found in the nature of

Christ. In Mark 10:37, we read where the two sons of Zebedee asked the Savior to grant them the privilege of sitting the one on his right hand and the other on his left in his glory. By the answer he made them as recorded in verse 40, the disciples understood him to make them promise of such positions, and in verse 41 we learn the ten were much displeased with James and John. Here we plainly discover an element of envy or jealousy in their nature. Thus they are found to be unlike their Savior in nature.

In reading the account of the betrayal in John 18, we see manifest an element of resentment and resistance when Peter with his sword smote off the high priest's servant's ear. Jesus commanded him to put up his sword. Elsewhere it is said that Jesus touched the wounded ear and healed it. Peter inflicted the wound; Jesus healed it. We see the dissimilarity in the natures of Peter and Jesus. The Savior, desiring the disciples to be restored to the divine nature, prays the Father to sanctify them: "Sanctify them through thy truth: thy word is truth."[8] While the disciples were only regenerated, we discover an element of division in their nature, resulting in disputings as to who should be the greatest, and envyings and jealousies, consequently they were not one; but in reading John 17:17-22, we find that the experience of sanctification makes them one. In Hebrews 2:11, we are taught that sanctification makes all one. When was this element of division destroyed or cleansed from the nature of the disciples? We answer, at the reception of the Holy Spirit at Pentecost. In Acts 4:31-32, it is said that all that were filled with the Holy Spirit were of one heart and one soul, consequently the experience of sanctification destroys all elements of division.

Paul rebuked the brethren for this same element of division that was found in the disciples before their sanctification. They were in Christ, but they had yet a carnal or fallen nature. In Acts 8, reading from verse 5, we have the account of Philip preaching Christ to the Samaritans. There were many lame and palsied healed, and evil spirits cast out. There was great joy in that city. In verse 12 it is said the people believed Philip preaching the things concerning the kingdom of God, and the name of Jesus Christ, and were baptized, both men and women. Verse 14 says that when the apostles at Jerusalem heard that Samaria had received the word of God, they sent Peter and John down there, who, when they were come, they prayed for them, and laid their hands on them, and they received the Holy Ghost. Here we find full salvation obtained by the people of the city of Samaria in the same manner as the apostles obtained it. They first received the word of God: they believed, and were baptized and were unquestionably regenerated, and like the apostles subsequently received the Holy Spirit.

In Acts 10 there is recorded how God wonderfully accomplished the sanctification of Cornelius and his family. We find him a devout man and one that feared God and prayed to Him always. His prayers and almsgiving came up as a memorial before God. How beautiful! Surely he was a Christian. He enjoyed the blessed experience of pardon, but not the glorious experience of sanctification; therefore, he was directed by an angel to call for one Simon who would tell him what to do. I would advise the reader to read the whole of this chapter. Toward the close of the chapter you will read where, as Peter preached to them, the Holy Ghost fell on them.

Thus we find that Cornelius and his family were fully saved in the same manner as the apostles and the people of Samaria. Some may be asking what was accomplished in these Gentiles when they received the Holy Spirit. We have already learned that He destroyed the elements of division and made all one. This is because he cleanses or purifies the nature or heart and consequently destroys all elements in opposition to the nature of Christ. We shall give one text to prove that the Holy Spirit purifies the heart: "And God, which knoweth the heart, bare them [Gentiles] witness, giving them the Holy Ghost, even as he did unto us [Jews]; and put no difference between us and them, purifying their hearts by faith."[9] With this one text all anti-cleansing theories fall to the ground.

In all the New Testament examples we find that men and women were first regenerated and subsequently made pure in heart by the sanctifying power of the Holy Spirit. This is the most natural and commonsense plan of restoring fallen man to his creative purity. Because of Adam's transgression sin entered into the world and death by sin; so death passed upon all men, for all have sinned (Romans 5:12). All have sinned. That is, all are sinful in their nature. This is proven by a saying of the Psalmist: "Behold, I was shapen in iniquity; and in sin did my mother conceive me."[10] The apostle Paul says he was by nature a child of wrath, even as others (Ephesians 2:3). He not only says he was a child of wrath in his nature, but that others are also.

This same is true of every child. The nature of the child in its formation in the womb is depraved. The moral condition of the parents may modify to an extent, but never wholly change that nature. The child does not inherit a depraved nature from its parents; it is not because the parents are sinful that the child is conceived in sin, but because nature is depraved. Understand me, Adam's sin caused a depravity in the whole realm of nature. The ground is cursed for his sake. Thorns and thistles shall it now bring forth. The world before sin's entrance was an Eden. Since, it is a land of sorrow, a world of vanity and woe. Man is of few days and full of trouble. It required a supernatural conception to beget a pure child, everything in nature being depraved. The child does not inherit either physical or moral image directly from its parents. In the protoplasm of human life there is implanted a physical and moral image. The child has two hands and two feet, not because its parents have, but because that is the form stamped by the hands of God in the embryo. Adam's sin struck at the root of nature, caused a change in the moral image implanted in the protoplasm of human life. When a child is born with two ears, eyes, hands, and feet, we say it is perfect in form, because that is the model stamped in the life germ. But should a child have six fingers upon one hand it is deformed, because it is not after the model. Adam's sin caused a deformity or depravity in the moral image in the life germ, and consequently every child is "conceived in sin," or in that deformed moral image. For this reason it required a conception from the supernatural world to beget the holy child Jesus. Because of this depravity in nature God's wrath hung over this world. We are all by nature children of wrath and doomed to eternal punishment had not Jesus presented Himself to the Father as a sacrifice for this depravity in nature. The sacrifice of the Son of God does not correct the deformity in nature (because after the sacrifice was offered the apostle declares we are by nature the children of wrath), we are yet evil in our nature, but the sacrifice of Christ appeases the wrath of God to the innocent. Praise God!

All children dying in their infancy are admitted into heaven through the sacrifice of Jesus. Some depart from the truth because they do not understand how the child can go to heaven and yet be depraved in its nature. They "do err, not knowing the scriptures, nor the power of God." The child is born with a depraved nature. This we have proved by Psalm 51:5; Ephesians 2:3, and it is also clearly proved by observation. Every child manifests an evil disposition. It comes natural for them to do evil things. Do they not learn evil things much more readily than right things? If so, why? Because their nature is evil. If one child is smitten by another, is it not natural for the injured one to smite back? All are compelled to answer, yes. If the child were pure in its nature such would not be the case. Christ was pure in His nature from infancy and had no disposition to resent injuries. A sanctified man is pure in his nature and has no disposition to return evil for evil.

This disposition is in the nature of children. Some have asked, "What is meant by *nature*?" It is not wise to follow too far and deep the insoluble things of God and nature lest we be led into error. The Scriptures, however, permit us to associate it with the heart, and it affects the whole of man. The Savior said, "Out of the heart proceed evil thoughts,"[11] which is the same as to say, out of man's nature proceed evil thoughts. When the Holy Spirit purified the hearts of Jews and Gentiles by faith (Acts 15:8-9), they received a purifying of their nature. An impure heart, and a depraved nature, are synonymous terms. But how can a child go to heaven and yet be depraved in its nature? Because the sacrifice of the Son of God has appeased the wrath of God against this deformity in nature. If children were given pure souls or natures at birth, as some do affirm, then all children that die in infancy go to heaven independently of a Savior; consequently there are myriads in heaven to whom the Savior is no Savior. This is contrary to the voice of Scripture.

Should the child depraved in its nature arrive to a knowledge of what was right and what was wrong and then willfully do the wrong it incurs the wrath of God, which is appeased only through repentance and the blood. When the wrath of God because of transgression is appeased by repentance and the blood the individual is returned to his childhood state; therefore Jesus says, speaking to the transgressor, "Except ye be converted, and become as little children, ye shall not enter into the kingdom of heaven."[12] Conversion restores man to the childhood state. Now it is the will of God that he be sanctified. Through the sacrifice of the Son of God he can obtain a correction of the depravity that was implanted in his nature by Adam's sin, and be made partaker of the divine nature. Now he is like Jesus and lives a Christian life naturally as He did. Praise God!

The purifying of man's nature or heart is necessary in order that he be not overcome and become a transgressor. Who has known a newly converted man to live year after year without being brought into transgression? The purifying of his heart places him where he for a lifetime is victorious over sin. Glory to our God! If a justified man dies before he receives knowledge of sanctification it is with him as with the infant. But for him to be a constant overcomer along the race of life he needs the cleansing of his nature and the power of the Holy Spirit. "This is the will of God, even your sanctification."[13] "And the very God of peace sanctify you wholly."[14]

---

1. John 1 (11) He came unto his own, and his own received him not. (12) But as many as received him, to them gave he power to become the sons of God, *even* to them that believe on his name: (13) Which were born, not of blood, nor of the will of the flesh, nor of the will of man, but of God.
2. Luke 6 (40) The disciple is not above his master: but every one that is perfect shall be as his master.

3. John 4 (17) The woman answered and said, I have no husband. Jesus said unto her, Thou hast well said, I have no husband:
4. Luke 6 (36) Be ye therefore merciful, as your Father also is merciful.
5. 1 John 3 (7) Little children, let no man deceive you: he that doeth righteousness is righteous, even as he is righteous.
6. John 3 (3) Jesus answered and said unto him, Verily, verily, I say unto thee, Except a man be born again, he cannot see the kingdom of God.
7. John 17 (22) And the glory which thou gavest me I have given them; that they may be one, even as we are one:
8. John 17 (17) Sanctify them through thy truth: thy word is truth.
9. Acts 15 (8) And God, which knoweth the hearts, bare them witness, giving them the Holy Ghost, even as *he did* unto us; (9) And put no difference between us and them, purifying their hearts by faith.
10. Psalm 51 (5) Behold, I was shapen in iniquity; and in sin did my mother conceive me.
11. Matthew 15 (19) For out of the heart proceed evil thoughts, murders, adulteries, fornications, thefts, false witness, blasphemies:
12. Matthew 18 (3) And said, Verily I say unto you, Except ye be converted, and become as little children, ye shall not enter into the kingdom of heaven.
13. 1 Thessalonians 4 (3) For this is the will of God, *even* your sanctification, that ye should abstain from fornication:
14. 1 Thessalonians 5 (23) And the very God of peace sanctify you wholly; and *I pray God* your whole spirit and soul and body be preserved blameless unto the coming of our Lord Jesus Christ.

PART II

1

CHRISTIAN CONDUCT

By the Word of God we have very briefly laid before the reader the plan of redemption, or how we are brought into the fullness of a Christian experience. Through repentance and faith by grace we receive pardon of all our transgressions and become as little children. Subsequently through consecration and faith by grace we are wholly sanctified or cleansed from an evil nature and made partakers of the divine nature. This is a restoration to the image of God. Man was created in God's image (Genesis 1:26-27). Through the sin of disobedience he lost the holy imprint of God's character in his soul and instead received the imprint of evil in his nature. Jesus came into the world to put away sin by the sacrifice of Himself, consequently through Him we are changed into the holy image of God again, "from glory to glory, even as by the Spirit of the Lord."[1] Praise God!

Now since we have come into the glorious fullness of God's salvation and bear His beautiful holy image in our nature and life, it now remains for us to show forth His glory and praise and life by bearing the excellent fruits of righteousness on to the end of our life's journey. "He that endureth unto the end shall be saved."[2] What can be more blessed than the privilege of walking with God in holiness, His peace and love streaming into our soul from His excellent glory and thrilling us with a tenderness and rapture known only by the redeemed? The harmonious uniting of the sweetest-toned instruments of music ever invented by man are only an empty sound compared with the sweet songs of redemption.

> *I'm redeemed and filled with glory;*
> *Streams of gladness from above*
> *Flowing, oh, so sweetly flowing,*
> *And my soul is full of love.*

The holy Bible is the book to guide the Christian's footsteps and govern his walk of life. When he walks in the truth, he walks even as Jesus walked; and when he strays from the truth, he departs from the life of Jesus.

You have heretofore agreed with me that a Christian life will naturally result from a Christian experience, and where the life is deficient the experience is also deficient. The Bible is the book by which our life is judged or graded. If we fall below one hundred per cent in any line of conduct, we fall that much below the standard of Christianity. It is not enough to live up to the Word of God in a few things, or in many things, but we must live according to the truth *in all things*. At the closing up of earthly scenes, you for your Christian experience must receive a general average of one hundred per cent to find admittance into the regions of eternal glory. If you are graded with a general average of only 99.9 per cent, you will hear the words, "Thou art weighed in the balances, and art found wanting,"[3] and may God help you to see.

A young lady recently said, after hearing a portion of the Scriptures read relating to practical Christianity, "Our preachers have not told us how to live." This remark occasioned the writing of this booklet. In the judgment day I desire to stand clear from the blood of all men. In the name of Jesus my Savior I shall do what I can to inform you how to live that you may please God and spend an eternity in the glory of His presence. Not only shall we tell you, but we shall earnestly pray to God for you.

The apostle Paul tells us in one short sentence how to live. He says, "Only let your conversation be as it becometh the gospel of Christ."[4] In other translations the word *conversation* is rendered *conduct*, which is a better rendering. In the Revised Version we have this rendering: "Only let your manner of life be worthy the gospel of Christ."[RV] A Christian life is one that becomes or adorns or makes beautiful the Word of God to the world. A holy and pure life is a jewel to crown the glorious gospel of Jesus. A Christian life is a light shining forth and revealing the gospel to a lost world. Oh, what a privilege granted unto us by grace that we can so live that our life magnifies the Word of God and makes it beautiful and attractive. Glory, glory be to our God!

With all my soul I appreciate the privilege of living a Christian life. We find many today who are disgusted with a professed Christianity, and disbelieve the Bible because of the imperfect lives of those who claim to be followers of the Lord Jesus. Many also, thank God, have been caused to believe the Bible and in the salvation of God by the pure and perfect lives of Christ's true and devoted followers, who walk as He walked. This is what is meant by living as "becometh the gospel,"[5] or, "[adorning] the doctrine of God."[6] By living a pure and holy life we interest others in the salvation of our God and His gospel. Praise God! To my soul this is such a beautiful point I am loath to leave it. The privilege of reflecting the glorious image of God to a darkened world by a pure life fills my soul with gratitude and praise. We have often seen a ray of sunlight passing from the keyhole through our darkened room and ending in a bright spot on the opposite wall. This reminds us of a Christian's life journey, which as a beautiful stream of light, finally ends in a bright spot upon the walls of time. By living upon God in prayer and holy thought, and by careful earnest effort, this light "shineth more and more unto the perfect day."[7] Every prayer and hour of holy meditation burnishes the image of God in our soul to a greater clearness and brilliancy. Every vagrant thought and hour of worldly meditation and gossip dims the features of the Christlikeness in our life, hence the exhortation, "Pray without ceasing."[8]

There is a way, an only way, that leads to eternal rest in the paradise of God. Jesus is the way, and He tells us to follow in His steps. The minister of a certain creed recently spoke of us in these words: "If they can do any good, very well, but I am not going that way." There is but one way (John 14:6; Jeremiah 32:39), and it is evident if he is not going our way he is not going to the same place. The Bible is the book given to guide us in the way. Who can persuade a man that he is not in the way that leads to the city when he is carefully following every signboard that points that way? Who can persuade a man he is not in the way that leads to eternal glory when he is carefully keeping every commandment of the Bible? "Blessed are they that do his commandments, that they may have a right to the tree of life, and may enter in through the gates into the city."[9]

Now we desire to give a few commandments teaching us what should be our daily manner of life. Paul in writing to Timothy said: "These things write I unto thee... that thou mayest know how thou *oughtest to behave thyself* in the house of God, which is the church of the living God, the pillar and ground of the truth."[10] Christian behavior is our theme. Had ministers everywhere been zealous to teach the whole of the commandments of God, and nothing but the commandments, no doubt our present task would be unnecessary. But the time has come (we speak the truth in love) when people with itching ears have heaped unto themselves teachers who have turned away from the truth and turned to fables, or the telling of amusing stories, consequently it becomes necessary that we be zealous to do what we can to declare the whole counsel of God. It is true, and sad that it is true, that from many pulpits and pews Christianity at this present day is reduced to almost nothing. In many religious organizations now extant there is but little to distinguish fair Christianity from the uncouth world. From the minister unto the most obscure layman they are jesting, talking foolishly, chewing and smoking, getting impatient and fretful, returning evil for evil, having enmity in their hearts against some fellow man, attending ball games, horse races, fox chases, etc.; engaging in politics, having membership in secret societies, loving money and laying up treasures on earth, neglecting to pay debts, etc.

Oh, what a shame! Is this not the ordinary life of many, many pretended followers of Jesus? Is this all there is of Christianity, which the Bible calls spotless and pure? We do not speak of these things to condemn you. God has not sent us into the world to condemn the world, but to preach the pure gospel, that the world might be saved. It is astonishing what little conception many a professed Christian has of Bible Christianity. They seem to think that church membership, church-going and giving, and a few outward ceremonies is all that is included in Christianity. One woman whom we met entertained hopes of heaven because she sent her children to Sunday school. Has Christianity been changed in its nature since the days of Jesus and the apostles? Is it any less to be a Christian now than it was then? Is not as much required of us today to be Christians as was required of the Christians in the first centuries of this gospel era?

With love and loyalty toward God we proceed to give a few Scriptures governing a Christian's daily life and practice.

---

1. 2 Corinthians 3 (18) But we all, with open face beholding as in a glass the glory of the Lord, are changed into the

same image from glory to glory, *even* as by the Spirit of the Lord.
2. Matthew 10 (22) And ye shall be hated of all *men* for my name's sake: but he that endureth to the end shall be saved.
3. Daniel 5 (27) TEKEL; Thou art weighed in the balances, and art found wanting.
4. Philippians 1 (27) Only let your conversation be as it becometh the gospel of Christ: that whether I come and see you, or else be absent, I may hear of your affairs, that ye stand fast in one spirit, with one mind striving together for the faith of the gospel;
5. Philippians 1 (27) Only let your conversation be as it becometh the gospel of Christ: that whether I come and see you, or else be absent, I may hear of your affairs, that ye stand fast in one spirit, with one mind striving together for the faith of the gospel;
6. Titus 2 (10) Not purloining, but shewing all good fidelity; that they may adorn the doctrine of God our Saviour in all things.
7. Proverbs 4 (18) But the path of the just *is* as the shining light, that shineth more and more unto the perfect day.
8. 1 Thessalonians 5 (17) Pray without ceasing.
9. Revelation 22 (14) Blessed *are* they that do his commandments, that they may have right to the tree of life, and may enter in through the gates into the city.
10. 1 Timothy 3 (14) These things write I unto thee, hoping to come unto thee shortly: (15) But if I tarry long, that thou mayest know how thou oughtest to behave thyself in the house of God, which is the church of the living God, the pillar and ground of the truth.

2

CHRISTIANITY IN HOME LIFE

Nowhere is Christianity more beautiful and blessed than in the home. It changes the home of wickedness, strife, and contention into a peaceful and delightful Eden. The home of the poor it converts into a palace. It drives away discontentment, uneasiness, fear, and darkness, and showers contentment, peace, assurance, and sunlight into every heart and home it is permitted to enter. Recently we saw some people shouting in a public meeting, and speaking in their testimonies of the blessedness of salvation. They said, "It is a heaven to go to heaven in." Yet in their homes we found them irritable, impatient, and contentious, which is very unlike heaven. But, thank God, Christianity brings a heaven to the home as well as in the public life. Christianity is Christ in the heart, and where Christ is, there is heaven; consequently a Christian has a heaven within him, and he has this heaven at home as well as abroad. Praise God!

Christianity in home life makes all peace, harmony, honesty, and faithfulness between master and servant; love and kindness between brothers and sisters; love and dutifulness between parents and children; love, trueness, and faithfulness between husband and wife. Christianity makes a home a heaven. Home where all is love and tenderness and devotion is the sweetest and most sacred spot on earth. A home where Christianity is crowned a queen in every heart is an Eden. The heart of God is filled with delight as he looks down upon such a home. His presence dwells there and causes this home to be a beautiful oasis in this desert world of sin. Alas, that such homes are so few! Sin destroys the happiness of man and makes many a home a hotbed of contention, strife, and confusion. Jesus came to put away sin and establish "on earth peace, good will toward men."[1]

---

1. Luke 2 (14) Glory to God in the highest, and on earth peace, good will toward men.

3

HUSBAND'S DUTY TO HIS WIFE

The Bible tells man what should be his behavior toward his wife, and a Christian must live and do just what the Bible says, without any modifications. The reader has already agreed with me that to have a Christian experience is to live a Christian life.

The husband is to regard the wife as the weaker vessel, and thus give her honor, support, and protection. "Likewise, ye husbands, dwell with them according to knowledge, giving honor unto the wife, as unto the weaker vessel, and as being heirs together of the grace of life; that your prayers be not hindered."[1] The husband must look upon his wife with respect, and because of her feminine sensitiveness have an especial care for her in spiritual things, and be her support in temporal things. Women have trials peculiar to their own sex, and a husband can scarce be called a husband, much less a Christian, that neglects to console and comfort them and throw as much joy and sunlight into their lives as possible. When Hannah wept because she had no son, her husband sought to comfort her with these words: "Why weepest thou? and why eatest thou not? and why is thy heart grieved? am not I better to thee than ten sons?"[2] May God help husbands to so dwell with their wives that when the wife is in discouragement and sorrow they can cheer them by recounting their love, devotion, and goodness to them—Why is thy heart grieved? am I not good and kind to thee?

Husbands must love their wives as themselves. "So ought men to love their wives as their own bodies. He that loveth his wife loveth himself. For no man ever yet hated his own flesh; but nourisheth and cherisheth it, even as the Lord the church."[3] The care Jesus exercises in nourishing and cherishing the church is illustrative of the care the husband should manifest in nourishing and cherishing his wife. "Husbands, love your wives, and be not bitter against them."⁴ All hasty, sharp, cross, unkind, cutting, bitter words are forever put away by the Christian husband, who loves his wife. Cross, hasty words are not the fruit of a Christian spirit; and if you have not ceased from them, God has better things for you.

---

1. 1 Peter 3 (7) Likewise, ye husbands, dwell with *them* according to knowledge, giving honour unto the wife, as unto the weaker vessel, and as being heirs together of the grace of life; that your prayers be not hindered.
2. 1 Samuel 1 (8) Then said Elkanah her husband to her, Hannah, why weepest thou? and why eatest thou not? and why is thy heart grieved? *am* not I better to thee than ten sons?
3. Ephesians 5 (28) So ought men to love their wives as their own bodies. He that loveth his wife loveth himself. (29) For no man ever yet hated his own flesh; but nourisheth and cherisheth it, even as the Lord the church:
4. Colossians 3 (19) Husbands, love *your* wives, and be not bitter against them.

4

WIFE'S DUTY TO HER HUSBAND

Nowhere is wickedness more greatly revealed than in a wicked woman, and nowhere is Christianity more beautifully exemplified than in a pure, chaste woman. "A virtuous woman is a crown to her husband."[1] "her price is far above rubies. The heart of her husband does safely trust in her.... She will do him good and not evil all the days of her life."[2] These words are beautiful and should encourage a wife to a life of faithfulness and devotion, that she may be a crown to her husband and be valued far above rubies. The wife that will honor and reverence her husband and seek to please him will find a joy in her own heart. "Her children arise up, and call her blessed; her husband also, and he praiseth her."³

Wives should love their husbands (Titus 2:4) and reverence them: "Let the wife see that she reverence her husband."⁴ The wife is to reverence her husband as the Christian reverences God. To reverence God is to be submissive to Him, and to look upon Him as our Lord and protector, adviser, etc.; to fear and obey Him, yet be in perfect freedom. Such should be the attitude of the wife toward her husband.

"Wives, submit yourselves unto your own husbands, as unto the Lord."⁵ Too few women comprehend the full meaning of this text. Just as the Christian consecrates, resigns, and submits himself to the care and control of God, so the wife is to submit herself to her husband. Just as the Christian leans in loving confidence upon God, so the wife should lean in loving confidence upon her husband; and the husband's conduct toward the wife should be such as would encourage her to trust and confide in him, as God's conduct toward us encourages us to trust and lean upon Him. When the husband and wife are kind, loving, and gentle toward each other, when she in her weakness feels her dependence upon him, and lovingly, trustingly looks unto him as her defense, and he in his strength and delight folds her in his strong arms of protection with a feeling of responsibility to nourish and cherish her—then they can testify that they have a heaven in their home. Unless they have attained unto such a life, they have not attained to a perfect Bible Christianity, neither to perfect joy and happiness.

---

1. Proverbs 12 (4) A virtuous woman *is* a crown to her husband: but she that maketh ashamed *is* as rottenness in his bones.
2. Proverbs 31 (10) Who can find a virtuous woman? for her price *is* far above rubies. (11) The heart of her husband doth safely trust in her, so that he shall have no need of spoil. (12) She will do him good and not evil all the days of her life.
3. Proverbs 31 (28) Her children arise up, and call her blessed; her husband *also*, and he praiseth her.
4. Ephesians 5 (33) Nevertheless let every one of you in particular so love his wife even as himself; and the wife *see* that she reverence *her* husband.
5. Ephesians 5 (22) Wives, submit yourselves unto your own husbands, as unto the Lord.

5

PARENTS' DUTY TO THEIR CHILDREN

Most parents believe they love their children, but true Christian love of parents toward children comprises more than many have understood. They may love them in a sense, but the parent that feels provoked toward the little one and threatens to slap it, calling it some ugly name, does not love the child with a Christian love. How many fathers and mothers under provocations are making severe threats to punish their children, at the same time calling them "ugly brats," "mean kids," "little imps," etc. Such parents are not Christians, no matter what may be their profession. They do not comprehend the true nature of Christianity if they believe themselves to be Christians while having such feelings and using such terms toward their children. Christianity is far more beautiful than this.

Parents are commanded to train their children up for God and heaven: "And, ye fathers, provoke not your children to wrath: but bring them up in the nurture and admonition of the Lord."[1] They must teach them God's Word: "Only take heed to thy self, and keep they soul diligently, lest thou forget the things which thine eyes have seen, and lest they depart from thy heart all the days of thy life: but teach them thy sons, and thy sons' sons."[2] "And ye shall teach them your children, speaking of them when thou sittest in thine house, and when thou walkest by the way, when thou liest down, and when thou risest up."[3]

They must tell them of the judgments of God, as given in His Word: "Tell ye your children of it, and let your children tell their children, and their children another generation."[4] Parents are to provide for their children: "But if any provide not for his own, and specially for those of his own house, he hath denied the faith, and is worse than an infidel."[5] Parents who through indolence fail to comfortably clothe and sufficiently feed and give them educational and religious advantages according to the Bible rule, such parents cannot be termed Christians. Parents cannot possibly be Christians and use their money for liquors, snuff and tobacco, and then fail to comfortably clothe and give their children a sufficiency of wholesome food, or fail to give them proper educational and religious advantages.

Now, elders and deacons are commanded to rule their children well and have them in subjection with all gravity (1 Timothy 3:4,12). Elders are an example to the flock; consequently it follows that all Christians must rule their children well and have them in subjection. Parents cannot have the approval of God on them, no matter how much they may pray and how active they may be in the religious life, if they allow their children to disobey them and go in the ways of sin. We have known many parents to pray for the salvation of their children, and all the while were allowing them to attend picnics, shows, parties, dances, etc. Such prayers go unanswered, and such conduct brings the wrath of God upon the parents. For the sake of your soul, and the souls of your children, restrain them from evil ways; prohibit them attending worldly places of amusement, but take them with you to the house of God. Great responsibility is laid upon the parents. They have a child whose eternal destiny depends largely upon the training it receives in youthful days. We would love to write much more on the subject, but must forbear, only adding these words of exhortation to every parent: As you value your and your children's eternal happiness in the glory of God's presence, get your soul fully saved and filled with love and the Holy Spirit so you can set a godly example before your children, and then seek help from God to train them up in the ways of righteousness.

---

1. Ephesians 6 (4) And, ye fathers, provoke not your children to wrath: but bring them up in the nurture and admonition of the Lord.
2. Deuteronomy 4 (9) Only take heed to thyself, and keep thy soul diligently, lest thou forget the things which thine eyes have seen, and lest they depart from thy heart all the days of thy life: but teach them thy sons, and thy sons' sons;
3. Deuteronomy 11 (19) And ye shall teach them your children, speaking of them when thou sittest in thine house, and when thou walkest by the way, when thou liest down, and when thou risest up.
4. Joel 1 (3) Tell ye your children of it, and *let* your children *tell* their children, and their children another generation.
5. 1 Timothy 5 (8) But if any provide not for his own, and specially for those of his own house, he hath denied the faith, and is worse than an infidel.

6

CHILDREN'S DUTY TO THEIR PARENTS

While it is the duty of the parent to teach his child, God makes it the duty of the child to heed the parent's teaching. "A wise son heareth his father's instruction."[1] Children are commanded to obey their parents: "Children obey your parents in the Lord: for this is right. Honor thy father and mother; which is the first commandment with promise."[2] Obedience to parents is well pleasing to God. "Children, obey your parents in all things: for this is well pleasing unto the Lord."[3]

Many boys and girls at the present day are found to utterly disregard their parents' commands and wishes. Such children have not yet experienced the power of regeneration, no matter how many societies and leagues they have membership in. Children, God holds you to love, honor, and obey your parents, and unless you do as He commands you have no promise of heaven.

---

1. Proverbs 13 (1) A wise son *heareth* his father's instruction: but a scorner heareth not rebuke.
2. Ephesians 6 (1) Children, obey your parents in the Lord: for this is right. (2) Honour thy father and mother; (which is the first commandment with promise;)
3. Colossians 3 (20) Children, obey *your* parents in all things: for this is well pleasing unto the Lord.

7

SERVANTS' DUTY TO THEIR MASTERS

We shall not use the word *servant* in the sense of a slave, but in the sense of a hired man or woman. They are to be subject to their employers (1 Peter 2:18); to obey them (Ephesians 6:5); to please them well in all things (Titus 2:9); should serve them with good will (Ephesians 6:7); should honor them (1 Tim. 6:1); must not defraud them (Titus 2:10); should be profitable unto them and do them good service (Philemon 1:11); should not serve them faithfully just to please man, but because it is right, in the sight of God (Ephesians 6:6; Colossians 3:22).

8

MASTERS' DUTY TO THEIR SERVANTS

About all we care to say on this subject is to condemn the evil of oppression. It is a disposition on the part of many to secure laborers at the lowest possible price. We shall give an illustration that will enable you to see the evil practiced by many who profess to love God and their fellow men.

Mr. A. is a laborer and a poor man. He goes to Mr. B. seeking employment. Mr. B. has work he desires to have done, but he wants it done at as low a cost as possible. Mr. A., in order to support his family, thinks he should have one dollar per day. Mr. B. does a little calculating and finds he could pay Mr. A. one dollar a day and make quite a profit, but he knows Mr. A. is a poor man and could probably only find work at even less wages, so he offers him seventy-five cents per day. Mr. A., rather than lose the job and be idle, consents to do the work at seventy-five cents, although, justly earning one dollar. What does the Scripture say? "Masters, give unto your servants that which is just and equal; knowing that ye also have a master in heaven."[1] And that "whatsoever ye would that men should do to you, do ye even so to them."[2] It is very sinful to refuse to pay one dollar per day to a laborer for his service when we know it is worth it, and that it would be just and right.

There is a disposition on the part of many employers to secure labor at just as low cost as possible, and a disposition on the part of the laborer to get as high price for his service as possible, consequently there is contention, quarreling, and bitter feeling between employer and employee, oftentimes resulting in strikes and serious trouble. Christianity removes all such trouble and makes everything just and equal. The Christian employee is willing to labor for that which is just and right, and the Christian employer is willing to give him that which is just and right, and thus all trouble is averted. Praise God!

1. Colossians 4 (*1*) Masters, give unto *your* servants that which is just and equal; knowing that ye also have a Master in heaven.
2. Matthew 7 (*12*) Therefore all things whatsoever ye would that men should do to you, do ye even so to them: for this is the law and the prophets.

9

CHRISTIANITY IN PUBLIC LIFE

There is one text which should rule the action of every man toward his fellow man. These are the words: "And as ye would that men should do to you, do ye also to them likewise."[1] We desire to mention a few sinful things we find practiced among men which reveal the wicked and selfish condition of the heart.

Many men are prone to misrepresent property they are offering for sale. For instance, a horse may be said to be seven years old by his owner when he knows he is ten. He may represent him to be sound in every way when he knows he is diseased, and for this very reason he desires to sell him. Of course, no man can do these things and be a Christian. The Bible says, "Lie not one to another."[2] "Wherefore putting away lying, speak every man truth with his neighbor."[3] The Christian not only tells the truth as is asked him concerning his horse, but he also tells of all his defects though he be unquestioned. If a horse should be in some way diseased or blemished unknown to and unsuspected by the purchasing party, the owner instead of seeking to hide his defect, frankly tells, if he is a Christian, all about the diseased and blemished condition. This is doing as he would be done unto, and is Christian conduct.

Recently a gentleman was telling me of a man who, when having his wheat threshed, asked the men that were doing the measuring to heap up the half bushel, that he might save some of his threshing bill. Is it not a pity that man will allow a covetous heart to lead him into such awful sin? He brings the wrath of God upon his soul for a few pennies. It is much worse than Esau selling his birthright for a mess of pottage. The salvation of Jesus saves men from such conduct; consequently a Christian desires the men to give a just and right measure, for under no circumstance would he defraud his neighbor, because he would not that men should do so to him. "By their fruits ye shall know them"[4]; so we know that a man that will thus defraud another is not a Christian.

Men sometimes become so greedy of gain that in order to secure the good price of an early market they will cut their melons when they have reason to believe they are too green. This is not Christian conduct, but is very sinful. It is not as you would want others to do to you, so let no man endeavor to persuade himself that he is a Christian when he has such a disposition of heart. Christianity is not merely a profession, but is an experience of the heart, and you have agreed with me that if a man has the experience he will live the life. Thus we are "known and read of all men."[5]

Sometimes men and women manifest a selfish and avaricious disposition at the counter of their grocer. They always want the grocer to give them down weight, just a few more ounces of meat, or a bit of sugar, or a few more inches of calico, etc. Of course, if the grocer is a Christian he will have patience with them and give them just weight and measure. Some people have the disagreeable custom of trying to get everything they buy at the very lowest price possible, and the highest price possible for everything they have to sell. This only indexes an impure heart. No matter to them if the merchant can only get 8 cents per pound for chickens in the city, they will want him to pay 8.5 cents, and would gladly take it if they could get it; and no matter to them if his calico cost him 5 cents per yard, they want it for 5 cents. This is all shameful and has led into sinful practices. Some excuse themselves for haggling unfairly with their merchant by saying, "He makes his goods too high, and we haggle with him to get him down to a reasonable profit." It is their practice of haggling unfairly that has forced the merchant into the practice of high marking. He expects you to haggle with him and so makes ready for you. This is wrong, and things ought not so to be. Farmers and mechanics have need of home merchants, and should be perfectly willing to allow their merchant a reasonable profit, and the merchant should not ask any more. Christianity sets these things right. It has come to pass that at the present time man has but little confidence in his fellow man. Christianity restores this lost confidence. Some of the leading men in the monopolies and "trusts" are professing to be followers of Jesus, and yet are hoarding up their thousands at the expense and cry of the poor. Such profession is an abomination to God. Christianity will break up all "trusts."

Christianity will compel a man to pay his debts if he possibly can. Refusing to pay debts is sinful and a Christian will not do such a thing. Christianity will not allow a man to place the inferior potatoes in the bottom of the barrel and the very finest on the top. In some sections of the country moneyed men have a custom of requiring a "bonus" on loaned money; that is, you borrow one hundred dollars of them and they want you to give a note for one hundred and ten dollars and give a legal interest besides. In the fear and love of God we say a Christian will not do such a thing. It is not doing as he would want others to do to him. It is oppressing the poor. The legal interest is all the law of the land and the law of God allows him, but he has forced the poor man to give him ten dollars for nothing, and he ought to be ashamed of such conduct. "Not every one that saith, Lord, Lord, shall enter the kingdom of heaven."[6]

Christianity will not allow a man to return evil for evil. If a Christian is smitten upon the right cheek he will turn the other. If his neighbor claims a few feet of land over the right line he will let him take it. If his neighbor abuses him and mistreats him he does him good in return. If his neighbor mistreats or kills any of his farm stock he in return will gladly rescue this neighbor's stock from injury. If this neighbor should set fire to his buildings he in return would put out a fire that was destroying his neighbor's buildings. If his enemy hungers, he feeds him; if he thirsts, he gives him drink. This is the spirit of Christianity as manifested in the life of Jesus, and as it was in Him so it will be in all who possess it. It is sometimes known that neighbors are at enmity with one another. Perhaps one or both of them profess to be Christians, yet they will not speak to each other if they meet upon the street or in their house of worship. Do you think that looks like Christianity? What shall they do in heaven should they get there? No, this is not Christian conduct, and any man that holds enmity or ill feelings, and ill wishes toward another fellow man and thinks he is a Christian is deceived, and I shall be thankful if this little book by the help of God's Spirit will help him out of his deception. Remember we are not writing for the purpose of condemning, but for the purpose of helping such ones to a real, living experience of salvation that will admit them into that glorious land of eternal rest when life's toils are over. Jesus says we should love our enemies, and pray for those who persecute us and despitefully use us (Matt. 5:44).

---

1. Luke 6 (31) And as ye would that men should do to you, do ye also to them likewise.
2. Colossians 3 (9) Lie not one to another, seeing that ye have put off the old man with his deeds;
3. Ephesians 4 (25) Wherefore putting away lying, speak every man truth with his neighbour: for we are members one of another.
4. Matthew 7 (20) Wherefore by their fruits ye shall know them.
5. 2 Corinthians 3 (2) Ye are our epistle written in our hearts, known and read of all men:
6. Matthew 7 (21) Not every one that saith unto me, Lord, Lord, shall enter into the kingdom of heaven; but he that doeth the will of my Father which is in heaven.

10

THE EFFECT OF CHRISTIANITY ON HABIT

Man in his sinful life often forms many habits that rule him. They grow upon him and gain such a power over him as to make him their slave. Some conclude it is no sin to indulge in certain habits as long as we do not go to an excess, and as long as we do not get into bondage. Indulgence to any extent whatever in bad habits is wrong. Swearing is a habit, and a bad one. Some men have so acquired the habit of swearing that they swear unconsciously. This excessive swearing is not only wrong, but any indulgence in such practice is wrong. Christianity breaks the power of such habits and sets man free. Such sin has no dominion over a Christian, not so much as a single indulgence. Men have formed the habit of drinking strong drink, using morphine and opium. They become slaves to these evil habits. Now it is not only a sin to indulge in them to an excess, but any indulgence in such evil practices is altogether unbecoming in a Christian. Some people have so lost sight of true Christianity that they think they can indulge in strong drink occasionally and yet be Christians approved of God. Such are laboring under a deception and will meet with a sad surprise in the judgment day. Christianity breaks the power of such evil habits and sets man free, so much so that they are not overcome by a single indulgence.

Many people have formed the habit of smoking and chewing tobacco and using snuff, and are so unconscious to the purity of a Christian life that they have never understood it to be wrong. Is it not surprising that man would attempt to worship God and gain heaven and indulge in such unclean practices? Now we do not mean to say anything harsh or unkind, for we pity all who are in bondage to such a hard master. We want you to see the evil of it and seek the Lord, who is able to set you free. Praise God! The using of tobacco is a habit, no one can deny this. The question is, is it a good or bad habit?! If it is a good habit we should advise all to form the habit. If it is an evil habit, we should advise all to cease using it. Any hygienic work condemns the use of tobacco. It is injurious to the human system. We are not our own. We should glorify God in our body and our spirit, which are His. God will hold man responsible for the care of his body. No one can abuse his own body and willfully injure his health without incurring God's displeasure. "Let us cleanse ourselves from all filthiness of the flesh and spirit, perfecting holiness in the fear of God."[1]

God will hold man responsible for the example he sets before the world, and before his own children. Where is the father that would give tobacco to his boy or girl? Most parents endeavor to keep it from their children, and some would even punish them were they to find them using it. How wrong it is to indulge in a thing forbidden to your children. Just to think of a Christian, a follower of Jesus, chewing and smoking and using snuff. A Christian is a light in this world; but what kind of a light is a tobacco user? Could he say to his children, "Follow me as I follow Christ"? Oh, may God help you to quit its use and live as becometh the gospel of Christ. We are to "adorn the doctrine of God our Saviour in all things."[2] A man chewing and spitting tobacco or using snuff is not a very beautiful adornment.

As I was driving through the country a few days ago I saw a farmer's wife emptying her husband's spittoon. She held it away out from her and turned her head as she turned it up. How shocking that a man would impose such a task upon his wife!

Again, God will hold a man responsible for the way he spends the money he has given him. Which is more beautiful in the sight of Christ or more becoming his life and gospel—to use money and chew and smoke it up, or take the money and give it to the poor? Surely we have said enough on this subject to convince every honest reader, so we shall leave it, praying God to bless you and to help you to live and obey the truth and all principles of righteousness.

---

1. 2 Corinthians 7 (1) Having therefore these promises, dearly beloved, let us cleanse ourselves from all filthiness of the flesh and spirit, perfecting holiness in the fear of God.
2. Titus 2 (10) Not purloining, but shewing all good fidelity; that they may adorn the doctrine of God our Saviour in all things.

11

CHRISTIANITY IN DRESS

The Bible, in telling Christians how to live, makes mention even of their dress. Why is this? It is because extravagance in dress is indicative of a proud heart. Thefts, murders, evil thoughts, pride, etc., come forth from the heart and defile the man (Mark 7:21-22). Any article of dress put on merely for adornment can only be the fruit of pride in the heart. Some may wear adornments by way of jewels, pearls, rings, necklaces, etc., and still say that they are not proud. But the Bible says, "By their fruits ye shall know them."[1] These facts are plain, no matter how much man or woman may deny them.

Some have asked, "Can I not be a Christian and continue to wear my rings and plumed hats?" We would ask, Can you be a Christian and willfully disobey the Word of God? What does God's Word say? "In like manner also, that women adorn themselves in modest apparel, with shamefacedness and sobriety; not with broided hair, or gold, or pearls, or costly array."[2] We have heard people say that this text does not mean what it says, or is not meant for us now. What makes you say that? It is because you do not want to live to it. If I should tell my daughter not to wear gold, and she continuing to wear it, and should tell others that I did not mean what I said, I should consider it an act of very great disrespect. Jesus says, "In my Father's house are many mansions: if it were not so, I would have told you. I go to prepare a place for you. And if I go and prepare a place for you, I will come again, and receive you unto myself; that where I am, there ye may be also."[3] Where is the professed Christian that does not believe that Jesus meant what He said in this text, or that He did not mean it for them? If He did not mean what He said in the former text or meant it for some other people, how can we know He meant what He said in the last text, or meant it for us? We all believe this text to mean what it says, and that it is meant for us. Why do we? Because we would love to have it that way. And why do some disbelieve the former text? Because they do not love to have it that way. Oh, the inconsistency of man! We shall quote this text in Timothy from the Syriac Version of the New Testament: "So also that women [dress] in chaste fashion of dress: and that their adorning be with modesty and chastity: not with curls, or with gold, or with pearls, or with splendid robes: but with good works as becometh women who profess reverence for God."

The curling of the hair, or the wearing of gold and pearls does not become a woman who professes reverence for God. Such things give them a worldly appearance. It is really painful to the Christian heart to see men and women laboring and planning and striving to keep up with the fashion. Someone has said, "We had just as well be out of the world as to be out of style." That is just what Christianity will do for you. It separates you from the world and its fashions and styles. Many a young man is driven to dishonesty merely to keep up with the world in its pride. His clothier perhaps goes unpaid while he walks the aisle of some fine meeting house with the air of a millionaire. He takes his part in the League or the Endeavor, and considers such service entitles him to the name Christian.

Many a husband is working hard to support his wife and children, while the wife is spending his hard-earned money for fashionable and costly array for herself and children. The new spring hats and bonnets must be purchased, and that in the latest style, if debts go unpaid. Many a mother is working late at night, and goes to her bed with an aching heart and head because of her desire to clothe her children after the world so they may attend Sunday school, etc. Oh, where is the plain and humble Christianity of primitive days! Let us take a look at the life of the lowly Nazarene and His devoted followers. Here we behold the humble and self-sacrificing Christian virtues.

While it is wrong and contrary to the Scriptures to spend money for gold and pearls and costly apparel, it is equally as wrong to make an unnecessary expenditure of money in the erection of buildings. When we see dwelling houses with their fancy carvings and domes and decorations, we conclude that vain is the heart of the owner; and when we see a meeting house with its towering steeple and stained windows, our heart is grieved. In the name of Jesus we affirm that it is wrong and contrary to the spirit of Christianity to make such an unnecessary expenditure of money in the building of a house of worship. We have seen many a meeting house that cost fully enough to build three plain houses that would seat as many people and fully as durable. The unnecessary expenditure of money in the building of these houses is often double the amount required to build a good comfortable plain building. Frequently meeting houses are remodeled when the old one was plenty good enough, but not fine enough. Why those colored windows with their drawings? Are they the result of love to God, or are they the result of pride? At this present writing there are thousands of human beings starving, not in foreign and heathen lands only— in our own beloved land many feel the pangs of hunger. With this suffering of human beings around us we say in the fear of God that no man nor society can expend money for costly colored windows and rich fancy carvings and ornamentation without incurring the displeasure of the Almighty.

Dear reader, I appeal to your commonsense and reason (if you do not know anything about the Bible): which is more congenial to the spirit of right and of Christianity and more commendable to God—to use money in buying feathered and flowered hats, laces, ribbons, necklaces, beads, jewels, gold rings, chains, studs, buttons, etc., or the giving of this money to some poor man or woman who is struggling hard to keep the wolf from the door? May God help us to see.

---

1. Matthew 7 (20) Wherefore by their fruits ye shall know them.
2. 1 Timothy 2 (9) In like manner also, that women adorn themselves in modest apparel, with shamefacedness and sobriety; not with broided hair, or gold, or pearls, or costly array; (10) But (which becometh women professing godliness) with good works.
3. John 14 (2) In my Father's house are many mansions: if *it were* not *so*, I would have told you. I go to prepare a place for you. (3) And if I go and prepare a place for you, I will come again, and receive you unto myself; that where I am, *there* ye may be also.

12

CHRISTIANITY SEPARATES FROM THE WORLD

Christians are not of this world. Jesus, in speaking of His followers, says, "If ye were of the world, the world would love his own: but because ye are not of the world, but I have chosen you out of the world, therefore the world hateth you."[1] The apostle John says: "Love not the world, neither the things that are in the world. If any man love the world, the love of the Father is not in him."[2] The apostle James says: "Ye adulterers and adulteresses, know ye not that the friendship of the world is enmity with God? Whosoever therefore will be a friend of the world is the enemy of God."[3] The apostle Peter says, "For the time past of our life may suffice us to have wrought the will of the Gentiles, when we walked in lasciviousness, lusts, excess of wine, revelings, banquetings, and abominable idolatries."[4] Salvation of God saves people from the sins of the world. The apostle Paul says: "Among whom [those who walked according to the course of the world] also we all had our conversation [conduct] in times past in the lusts of our flesh, fulfilling the desires of the flesh and of the mind, and were by nature the children of wrath, even as others."[5] When he was in sin he walked as the world walked, but when he became a Christian he was saved, or separated, from such a life. The spirit of Christianity and the spirit of the world are directly opposite in their nature. "What fellowship hath righteousness with unrighteousness?"[6]

Surely every reader is convinced that Bible Christianity saves men and women from a worldly life. Now how is the world going? We see them striving, planning to lay up treasures here upon earth. Christian conduct is to lay up treasures in heaven. We see the world joining secret societies and trusting in life insurances for protection. Christians with any degree of light do not do such things, but trust wholly in God, who has promised to care for them. We see the world dressing in feathers, flowers, laces, ribbons, beads, pearls, jewels, gold, and costly array. Such is not the Christian's dress. They are commanded to dress in modest apparel with shamefacedness, as people should who profess godliness. We see the world chewing and smoking tobacco and using snuff, opium, etc. Such is not Christian conduct, neither is it becoming to the gospel of Christ. We as Christians must live clean, pure and holy lives.

We see the world trusting in omens and signs, or a kind of witchcraft, such as a horseshoe bringing good luck, and hundreds of other very foolish signs very unbecoming a Christian, but is a fruit of the flesh (Galatians 5:19-21). We see the world returning evil for evil; when wronged they seek revenge. Christians do not act that way; they love their enemies. They are not overcome with evil, but overcome evil with good. We see the world engaging in foolish and slangy talk, the telling of stories, and saying funny and amusing things. Such is not a godly nor Christian conversation. Christians are to be sober minded, to have a sound speech; every word must be seasoned with grace, that it may minister grace to the hearers.

We see the world going to shows, fairs, picnics, card parties, ball games, horse-races, theaters, etc. Christians do not love the world nor its revelry.

There is too much for a lover of the Lord to do in this sinful world to spend time in such worldly amusements; besides he has no desire for such things. His affections are set on things above. What do you think of a professed Christian sitting along side of a worldly man watching the horse-races? When the race is becoming very close they both get nervous, and both cheer with equal enthusiasm. What kind of a light is this professed Christian? What is there here noble or beautiful for Christianity? While the professed Christian and his unprofessed companion are cheering over the horse-race the true Christian is visiting the sick, or encouraging the discouraged, or helping the needy, or about his honest toil.

The reader can at once see which is more Christ-like. I pray God to make every professed Christian who thus enjoys the world to blush with shame as he reads this. Sometimes we see a company of young men and young women walking down the street, maybe the greatest number of them belong to church, and it goes out before the world that they are Christians, but along with their unprofessing companions they are jesting and laughing, and giddy and frivolous, and fashionably dressed, so you cannot tell the life of the one from the other. Ah, tell me where is the separation between the Christian and the world if this be Christianity.

Alas! how sad that the standard of Christianity has been so lowered that you are in many instances unable to distinguish it from the world. Thank God! true Christianity retains her exalted seat far above this world. She reigns a queen of light and peace in her robes of spotless white. She is beautiful. "She... looketh forth as the morning, fair as the moon, clear as the sun, and terrible as an army with banners."[7]

---

1. John 15 (19) If ye were of the world, the world would love his own: but because ye are not of the world, but I have chosen you out of the world, therefore the world hateth you.
2. John 2 (15) And when he had made a scourge of small cords, he drove them all out of the temple, and the sheep, and the oxen; and poured out the changers' money, and overthrew the tables;
3. James 4 (4) Ye adulterers and adulteresses, know ye not that the friendship of the world is enmity with God? whosoever therefore will be a friend of the world is the enemy of God.
4. 1 Peter 4 (3) For the time past of *our* life may suffice us to have wrought the will of the Gentiles, when we walked in lasciviousness, lusts, excess of wine, revellings, banquetings, and abominable idolatries:
5. Ephesians 2 (3) Among whom also we all had our conversation in times past in the lusts of our flesh, fulfilling the

desires of the flesh and of the mind; and were by nature the children of wrath, even as others.
6. 2 Corinthians 6 (14) Be ye not unequally yoked together with unbelievers: for what fellowship hath righteousness with unrighteousness? and what communion hath light with darkness?
7. Song of Solomon 6 (10) Who *is* she *that* looketh forth as the morning, fair as the moon, clear as the sun, *and* terrible as *an army* with banners?

13

WHAT CHRISTIANS MUST NOT DO

- They must not steal (Ephesians 4:28).
- They must not lie (Ephesians 4:25).
- They must not return evil for evil (1 Thessalonians 5:15).
- They must not talk foolishly (Ephesians 5:4).
- They must not speak idle words (Matthew 12:36).
- They must not dress in gold, or pearls, or costly array (1 Timothy 2:9-10; 1 Peter 3:3-4).
- They must not get angry (Ephesians 4:31).
- They must not murmur (Philippians 2:14).

- They must have no fellowship with the unfruitful works of darkness (Ephesians 5:11).
- They must not love the world (1 John 2:15-17).
- They must not engage in idolatry, witchcraft, hatred, variance, emulations, wrath, strife, seditious, heresies, envyings, murders, drunkenness, revelings, nor such like (Galatians 5:20, 21).
- They must not speak evil of any man, and be no brawlers (Titus 3:2).
- They must not be lovers of self, proud, boasters, covetous, disobedient, unthankful, unholy, fierce, despisers of the good, heady, highminded, nor lovers of pleasure (2 Timothy 3:2-4).

In short, they must not be nor do anything the Word of God says they must not be nor do.

14

WHAT CHRISTIANS MUST DO

- They must love God (Mark 12:30).
- They must obey him (Acts 5:29).
- They must love their enemies, and pray for them (Matthew 5:44).
- They must be meek and gentle (Titus 3:2).
- They must be kind and tenderhearted (Ephesians 4:32).
- They must be merciful (Luke 6:36).
- They must do to others as they would that others should do to them (Luke 6:31).
- They must count it joy when they fall into temptations (James 1:2).

- They must abstain from all appearance of evil (1 Thessalonians 5:22).
- When smitten on the right cheek they must turn the other (Luke 6:29).
- They must have a sound speech (Titus 2:8).
- They must deny self (Matthew 16:24).
- They must be a light (Philippians 2:15).
- They must pray without ceasing (1 Thessalonians 5:17).

In short, they must keep all the commandments of the New Testament.

We therefore kindly advise everyone to search the Scriptures, that you may know what God requires of you.

CHRISTIANITY

Christianity—Stately Queen—
Virgin—loveliest ever seen,
Fairest art thou upon the earth,
And of a nobler, higher birth.
When King Agrippa heard
    thy name
And how abroad was spread thy
    fame,
And saw thee, lovely as thou art,
Thou almost won his heathen
    heart.
When bound in dungeon's cruel
    stock
Thou gavest earth one mighty
    shock,

*The prison-keeper felt thy power,
And trembling in the midnight
　hour,
Fell humbly at thy feet and craved
A knowledge how he could be
　saved;
Thou didst send pardon from
　above,
In turn he washed thy stripes in
　love.
When kneeling down beside
　the dead
In solemn accents thou hast said,
"Dorcas, in Jesus' name arise";
When opened were the woman's
　eyes,
By gentle hand thou led her forth,
A monument of thy great worth.
Weeping beside the dead man's
　tomb,
With a loud voice thou bid'st him
　"come,"
Though he four days in death had
　lain,
Thou call'dst him back to life
　again.
When beside the Beautiful gate,*

*Where halt and maimed for alms
 did wait,
To one who from his birth was
 lame,
Thou did'st say, "Arise in Jesus'
 name";
And he by trusting in thy word
Arose and leaped and praised the
 Lord.
When woman did her sin deplore;
Thou whispered, "Go and sin no
 more."
A palsied man thy power would
 know,
Then was he healed, washed as
 white as snow.
When Simon saw thy wondrous
 power,
He sought to win thee with a
 dower,
Within his wicked heart he
 thought
Thy fame with money could be
 bought;
But earthly treasures glittering
 bright
Are worthless in thy virtuous sight:*

*Thou spurned his offer, and
 made bold
To bid him perish with his gold.
So pure art thou, O Christian fair,
No sin can thine own presence
 bear;
They lied to thee and lost their life,
Both Ananias and his wife.
A rich man with a haughty heart,
From out his gate bid thee depart;
He loved his wealth, but one day
 dies—
In hell he lifted up his eyes.
A beggar full of pains and aches,
Thy offered hand in welcome
 takes;
Enduring pains he one day dies—
Is borne by angels to the skies.*

*Fairest art thou 'mong the fair,
Thy graces none but thee can wear;
As bridegroom decked with
 ornaments,
Or bride with jeweled hyacinths,
So thou adorned in robes of white
Art on the earth a gleam of light.
Thy cheeks are comely as the rose,*

*Thy neck as white as winter
 snows,
Thy lips are like a scarlet thread,
Thy locks like silver on thy head,
Thy fingers set in diamond rings,
Thy voice in sweetest music sings;
Thy teeth are like an ivory ball,
Thy stature like the palm tree tall;
Thou art more gentle than the
 dove;
To him who with thee is in love,
No spot or blemish can there be,
Fair Virgin, found at all in thee;
With crowns of glory on thy brow,
Beauty's perfection, Maid, art
 thou.
With thy banner of love unfurled,
On thy mission throughout the
 world
Thou goest, scattering precious
 seeds
Of gentle words and kindly deeds
To the sad heart and troubled
 breast,
Thou bringest peace and joy and
 rest,
Man's humble home is truly blest,*

When thou art crowned a royal
    guest;
Sorrow and sighing flee away
On that sweet coronation day.
Thy beauty more and more I see.
Thy love grows dearer unto me;
My heart thy throne, oh, let it be
Through life, and when I've
    reached the end.
Together let us quick ascend
To heaven's bright and shining
    shore,
There dwell together evermore.

Copyright © 2021 by Alicia Editions
Cover Design: Canva.com
All rights reserved.

www.ingramcontent.com/pod-product-compliance
Lightning Source LLC
LaVergne TN
LVHW040157080526
838202LV00042B/3202